MASQUERADE

I AM THE KEEPER OF
THE JEWEL OF
MASQUERADE
WHICH LIES WAITING
SAFE INSIDE ME
FOR YOU
OR ETERNITY

KIT WILLIAMS

MASQUERADE

THE COMPLETE BOOK
WITH THE ANSWER EXPLAINED

Within the pages of this book there is a story told
Of love, adventures, fortunes lost, and a jewel of solid gold.
To solve the hidden riddle, you must use your eyes,
And find the hare in every picture that may point you to the prize

WORKMAN PUBLISHING
NEW YORK

Library of Congress Cataloging in Publication Data

Williams, Kit.
Masquerade, the complete book
with the answer to the riddle.

Summary: Presents the original text and illustrations
with an explanation of the clues and how they led
to the discovery of the treasure.
1. Literary recreations. 2. Picture puzzles. 3. Treasure-trove.
[1. Literary recreations. 2. Riddles. 3. Buried treasure] I. Title.
GV1493.W48   1983   793.73   82-40502
ISBN 0-89480-369-7 (pbk.)

Publishing History
Hardcover edition originally published in 1979 by Jonathan Cape,
30 Bedford Square, London, England. Hardcover edition
published in the U.S.A. in 1980 by Shocken Books, New York.
Paperback edition first published in 1982 by Jonathan Cape,
and published here by arrangement with Jonathan Cape.

The names of the people without whom
Masquerade would not have been published
are incorporated in the pictures. To these
the artist would like to add Rupert Lancaster.

Kit Williams' original works of art are exhibited
exclusively by Portal Gallery Ltd., London, England.

Workman Publishing
1 West 39 Street
New York, New York 10018

Printed in Italy by
Arnoldo Mondadori Editore, Verona

First printing March 1983
10 9 8 7 6 5 4 3 2 1

INTRODUCTION

I T ALL BEGAN in 1976 when Tom Maschler, Chairman of the publishers Jonathan Cape, came to see me. He had seen my paintings at the Portal Gallery in London and wanted to know if I would illustrate a children's book. *Illustrate* a children's book! I explained I was a painter and not an illustrator, and anyway I wouldn't want to draw pictures for someone else's story. So he suggested I write a story of my own. I'd never written anything in my life, and so I said "no" to that too. He left saying, "I bet you can do something with books that no one has ever done before." And those words stuck in my mind.

One day some weeks later, an idea came to me while I was eating breakfast, but I told it to go away. I was much too busy to be bothered with ideas for books. Then I started thinking about what books are and how they work. By dinner time that first idea was back with a friend, and soon the whole room was full of ideas. I couldn't resist the thought of a book that a lot of people would want to examine closely. I rang up Tom Maschler and said I would need £3,000 to do it. He didn't seem to understand completely how it would work but he very bravely sent me a contract straight away.

What I wanted to do was to retain the format of a book but then do something different. If I was going to spend two or three years doing sixteen paintings, I didn't want them to be just flicked through and put down. That's why the perspective is odd in some of the *Masquerade* pictures, and why others overlap their borders. Sometimes things come straight out at you. All to make you look really closely. The riddles and the treasure are also partly to make people look. Little did I know how hard they were going to look!

When I was a child there were competitions on cereal packets that pretended to be treasure hunts. They always seemed such disappointing gimmicks because the puzzles weren't exciting and the treasure wasn't worth the hunt. I thought I would do something for my lost childhood and make a real treasure from gold, bury it in the ground, and use riddles to lead people to it.

I did various experiments with map co-ordinates and bits of string in fields but I couldn't find a simple and accurate way to pinpoint the treasure. It would have to be marked by something already there. A monument, for example. I've always been fascinated by astronomy and I worked out a way of using a monument like the upright pointer on a sundial. The treasure could be buried where the end of the shadow was on a certain day in the year. I liked the idea of the equinox because it gives you two days each year, spring and autumn, when the shadow is exactly the same length. I remembered visiting a place called Ampthill Park when I lived near Bedford, where there's a cross about 18 feet high commemorating the first of Henry VIII's six wives, Catherine of Aragon. When I went to Ampthill to check everything would work, I found a small stone a few yards away from the cross with these words from Psalm 104 on it:

> O Lord how manifold are thy works!
> in wisdom hast thou made them all:
> the earth is full of thy riches.

That settled it. Ampthill was the perfect place. It wasn't famous for anything – then! Catherine of Aragon introduced lace-making to Bedfordshire, and the rhyme "Jack be nimble, Jack be quick", which I used for Jack Hare in the Isaac Newton picture, is an old lace-makers' song. And Jonathan Cape's address is *Bedford* Square, so the name of the nearest big town would be printed in every copy of the book.

Solving the master riddle that pointed to where the treasure could be found should depend on a relationship of words *and* pictures. I wrote out a sentence of about twenty words defining exactly, to within a few inches, where the gold would be buried. Once I had that sentence, I worked out how to put it into the construction of the pictures. All I had in mind for a story when I began to paint was the idea of a messenger going through the elements of earth, air, fire and water. The hare fitted because it isn't a cuddly animal, like a rabbit, and it can run very fast.

For me the crucial picture was the one which appears first in the book. I had been painting all day every day, even at weekends, becoming more and more obsessed and inward-looking. It was December, and the combination of the fumes from my paraffin heater in the workshop and the water dripping on the polythene tent I'd built to keep condensation off while I worked was driving me slightly crazy. At night I spent hours staring at the moon through my telescope and observing the moonlit landscape so that during the day I could convey the quality of moonlight in the painting. It was then that the story came to me: the hare should be the messenger of the moon. Only later did I discover that the hare is a messenger in legends and folklore in many countries.

Each of the pictures in *Masquerade* is like a big fat novel: there are plots and sub-plots and things going on that aren't even hinted at in the text. And I enjoyed putting in some personal jokes too: the names Lionel Levy and Eric Lister, which appear in "Jack in the Green", are the names of the owners of the Portal Gallery where I exhibit my paintings, and Tom Maschler's name is on the removal van in the aerial view of Tewkesbury. I was painting the man drinking tea on Silver Jubilee Day, and so I put the Queen's head on the tea caddy. The little girl with the Penny-Pockets Lady is the daughter of the chemist in my village, and I painted her as the girl swimming, as I imagine she'll look when she's sixteen.

Some things came out of the pictures to fit the story in an almost magical way. I'd just finished the paintings of Isaac Newton and the puppet on the beach at the end of the book when a friend showed me the quotation on Isaac Newton's statue in Cambridge: "All my life I seem to have been only like a boy playing on the sea-shore . . ." It fitted perfectly, so I put it in the story. The girl who worked at the gold merchant's in Birmingham where I bought the gold was called Dawn, so I thought I'd write her into the story where the moon makes the jewel "with a little gold taken from the dawn sky". I wonder if she's ever read the book!

Writing the text only took about three weeks as I already had it clear in my head. Now I had to make the jewel and bury it. I had never made jewellery, although I'd worked in brass, steel and copper. My methods were unsophisticated and sometimes unconventional, using old-fashioned tools, like an Archimedes drill. From one piece of gold I cut the outline of the hare, five and a half inches from nose to tail, then sawed out and drilled the filigree work within the body. The other piece of gold was enough to make the hare's legs, ears and tail, which I riveted to the body. Everything else – the bells and their tongues, the chains, the tiny animals – had to be made by melting down the remaining scraps of gold, beating them into coin shapes, then cutting them out.

The stones I chose were a ruby for the hare's eye, turquoise in the flowers on the body and a large moonstone for the back of the moon. The faces of the sun and moon are made of faïence, a substance the ancient Egyptians used a lot. I had to experiment for ages because the facial expressions changed so much as the faïence cooled and hardened.

The first time I gave the whole thing a good polish it looked a bit plain in some places, so I engraved the gold with tools my grandfather, a gunsmith, had left me. Though the gold and precious stones cost less than £1,500, the pendant was valued at £5,000 when I'd finished it. I suppose it must be worth a small fortune now.

I also had to make a special container out of clay in the shape of a hare. I engraved the words "I am the keeper of the jewel of Masquerade which lies waiting safe inside me for you or eternity" on the side of the pot and fired it in a kiln. Then, under the lights of television, I wrapped the gold in paper, put it in the pot, poured in hot wax and put on the lid. As the wax cooled it hardened and sealed the jewel in. It was very moving.

On the night of August 7th, 1979, I set off with Bamber Gascoigne, who was chosen to witness the burial. Once at the right spot, I cut a turf about ten inches square with my knife, then dug down until I'd made a hole to the depth of my elbow. There was a moment of panic when my trowel hit rock, but it turned out to be just a small stone. In went the pot with the gold, then the earth and the turf. I watered the spot to encourage the grass to grow again. As Bamber and I shook hands over the burial ground, the moon came out from behind a cloud and, I like to think, shone down a blessing on us.

Six weeks later the book was published and the world went crazy! People seized on everything I had put in the book and lots of things I hadn't. One poor woman had her garden invaded as people spotted the topiary hare in the aerial view of Tewkesbury. A man hid in the grounds at Sudbury Hall in Derbyshire (which is the swimming girl picture) so that he could dive in the lake in front of the house after dark.

Sudbury Hall is an example of the strange coincidences which seem to surround *Masquerade*. I painted the house from an old photograph – I've never been there – taken before the white dome was gilded. Treasure hunters were intrigued to find it was actually gold. And there is a stone frog in the grounds, just like the one I put in the shop window picture. To make people even more certain they were on the right track, there happened to be an exhibition of marionettes and toys there when *Masquerade* was published. The organizers of the exhibition had fun arranging alphabet blocks in the display to spell out other places near by so that treasure hunters wouldn't dig up the grounds.

All these stories I heard secondhand – or read about in newspaper articles. Very soon I had my own evidence of what I'd started. Letters began to pour in. I had phone calls in the middle of the night and muddy people carrying spades turned up at my door. One man wrote to me from Switzerland to say that his family had urged him to spend their savings on a journey to England, where he ended up on a remote and dangerous clifftop in Cornwall. Taking his life in his hands, he had shinned down the cliff face, and then got cut off by the incoming tide. A woman who wrote asking me to pay her fare to somewhere else in the British Isles actually lived only a mile from where the treasure was buried. Someone was even convinced he could reach the treasure if he found out my real name. Kit Williams, he declared, was just an anagram of "I will mask it".

Then suddenly, on Friday February 19th, 1982, a map turned up in the post which changed everything. We were woken up, as usual, by the dog barking at the postman and my wife Eleyne went down to get the letters and make the tea. Besides two fat parcels of letters from America, there were six letters Eleyne recognised as coming from known *Masquerade* treasure-hunters, and another one which she brought upstairs. I opened it as casually as I'd opened thousand upon thousand in the past. There it was, a letter with a map like a child's drawing, but enough for me to know someone had cracked it.

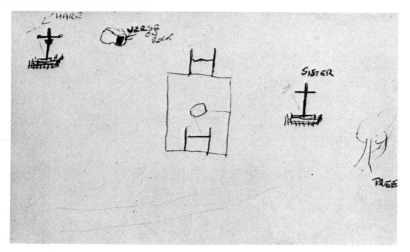

I felt elated and relieved. That simple drawing would prove to everyone that it was not impossible to find the jewel. The letter was just signed "Ken". I'd always promised to contact anyone who discovered the burial place. I leapt out of bed, rang the number in the letter and asked for Ken. When I told him his solution was correct, he said he couldn't dig it up that day because he had a cold. Not the reaction I'd expected!

Ken became really excited later in the day when he phoned back and explained how he'd found the spot which had eluded everyone else. He had been on the search for nearly eighteen months. Early on, he had arrived at Catherine of Aragon from ONE OF SIX TO EIGHT under the first picture in the book. He decided this was an important clue and did some research into her life. He made hundreds of expeditions to Kimbolton Castle in Cambridgeshire, where she died. He also believed from the Dance in Time picture that the equinox was important for measuring distance.

The clever bit – though it short-circuited my method – was to spend a lot of time investigating my own life and discovering I had lived near Bedford and in Kent. Even so, the search got nowhere. Twice he gave the book away, and each time went out to buy another copy to begin all over again.

One day when he was driving home, he decided to stop to give the dog a run and turned off the road at Ampthill Park. He didn't know then that a monument to Catherine stood there. It was the dog who discovered the stone with the "All the riches of the earth" verse on it. Could this be it? That night, he read in the *Shell Guide* that one of the pair of stone crosses he'd been looking at in the afternoon had been put up in honour of Catherine of Aragon in 1773. That settled it. He was sure that providence and his dog had led him to the buried treasure.

For three nights Ken tried to get underneath that stone, convinced the treasure lay there. But it wouldn't budge. He then concentrated on Catherine's Cross instead. He was a bit worried by what he thought were signs of digging near the cross, but it only made him more certain he was in the right place. Remembering the equinox, he got a friend to help him work out how the sun would cast a shadow of the cross on any particular day. He dug a small hole and found nothing. It was at this point he sent me the map for confirmation.

When he next went back to the site he got a real shock. A fresh hole had appeared close by. He dug like crazy until he was standing in a trench 8 feet long and 2 feet wide. Still there was no sign of the treasure. Next day Ken checked his measurements and found they led to the middle of his trench. By now he was convinced someone had already dug up the treasure. There seemed to be no alternative to announcing that an unknown person had found the treasure and kept quiet about it.

On Tuesday morning, four days after I'd received his letter, Ken rang again. "Look, don't tell the press yet. What if someone went along with a metal detector where I dug and found it? I'd feel a real Charlie. I might have missed it in the dark." Ken's plan was to go back in the *daytime*, pretending to be a workman. He went prepared with some poles and tape, put up a makeshift fence and dug again, in full daylight. He told passers-by he was investigating subsidence.

I was at a friend's house on Wednesday, February 24th when Eleyne rang to say there had been a new development. "I think you should come home." New development? I thought Ken must have been arrested! I rang him up. He'd found it – at a quarter to three that afternoon. What a relief! Apparently the casket had been just under the surface where he'd dug at night. He had missed it in the dark and reburied it. The sun was shining for the first time for days, and the shadow of the cross was very clear. I love the idea of the moon shining on the burial and the sun shining as it was unearthed. As Ken filled in the hole, the Bedfordshire Army Cadet Corps came along for training. Ken soon had them marching up and down his trench to firm the soil back in!

Ken wanted me to be there when he took the golden hare out of its casket and was happy to wait until arrangements were made to record the momentous event. But the following day no one could get through to him. Had he just disappeared with the jewel in fright? So far, I hadn't either seen the casket or checked the site for myself. How could I be sure Ken had actually found it?

For once the explanation turned out to be simple. He had been

taken suddenly into hospital. An illness that bothered him from time to time had been aggravated by all those nights of digging. He'd be out again in about a week. We agreed to meet as soon as he got back home. Days of suspense followed. Then at last, on Sunday, March 7th, Tom Maschler and I drove out to see him.

As the world now knows, Ken had the jewel all right, and we planned the day of announcement over a glass of whisky in Ken's cottage. For personal reasons, he wanted to retain his anonymity and agreed to speak to one newspaper and one television programme, but afterwards to vanish from the limelight. It was only right to respect his wishes. He said he wouldn't think of selling the golden hare – not for some years anyway. He'd spent eighteen months looking for it and wouldn't be parted from it now.

The thing Ken hadn't unravelled was the master riddle I'd hidden in the book. He had discovered some important clues, so it wasn't just a fluke that he'd found the jewel. He'd got some of the confirmers as well. The word CULMINATION on the border to the last picture in the book, for instance, meant originally "to be on the meridian" – the point where the sun is at its highest in the sky. The shadow cast by the cross at the time of the equinox would be accurate to the inch. Ken saw through some of my red herrings too. Many people have spent hours on the numbers in the football pitch in the aerial picture of Tewkesbury, but Ken, who is an engineer, recognised them as atomic numbers for chemical elements. Translated into letters, they spell: FALSE NOUU THINK AGAIN. Of all the people who wrote to me, a girl of twelve was one of only four to see this.

I didn't tell Ken how to get the rest of it. It seemed a shame to spoil the fun for everyone else by announcing how to crack the code before anyone had managed to work it out. But a letter from a teacher in Manchester, which arrived at my home just as this paperback edition of the book was going to press, changed all that. He was the one who had sent Ken into a frenzy by digging a hole near by at Ampthill. Failing to find the treasure on that dig,

Mike and his friend John had decided to wait – too long as it turned out – for the equinox on March 20th to pinpoint the spot. Still, the quest had been fulfilled, for theirs was the first completely correct solution to reach me.

It had taken them less than a year to solve it and they first reconnoitred the site in January 1982. Mike returned with his wife to dig their hole on the night of February 18th, when Ken's letter to me was safe in the post. They were in no doubt they had the right answer and wrote to me after hearing the news about Ken's discovery.

All the clues I've ever given are in this book, including the drawing I did for the *Sunday Times* at Christmas 1980. I dare you not to turn straight to the last page before you've tried to work it out for yourself. Don't overlook the significance of the Isaac

Newton picture and remember that, once you've spotted the method, you must apply it in turn to all fifteen framed pictures and the words around them. The story only contains confirmers. You should end up with nineteen or twenty-two words, depending on how you look at it. Those words tell you where to go and what to do.

When you think you know the answer, turn to the back and see how Mike and John got it right, and yet missed finding the golden hare by a whisker.

Gloucestershire
March 1982

KIT WILLIAMS

Once upon a perfect night, unclouded and still, there came the face of a pale and beautiful lady. The tresses of her hair reached out to make the constellations, and the dewy vapours of her gown fell soft upon the land.

Each picture in this book has a hare in it somewhere.
Can you find him in this picture?

AS OLD AS EARTH

AND IN THE EARTH AM I

I AM AS COLD AS EARTH

ONE OF SIX TO EIGHT

This lady, whom all mortals call the Moon, danced a merry dance in the pathless sky, for she had fallen in love, and the object of her devotion was the Sun.

Although all happiness was in her dance, there was also a little sadness, for whenever the dance led her into the same part of the sky as the Sun, she seemed to simply fade away, and feared the Sun might never notice her.

The Sun, for his part, and contrary to his appearance, was always sad. The one thing he wished for most was a friend. But when people looked at him they immediately screwed up their faces and turned away, which made the Sun think that he must be terribly ugly.

On this night the lady of the pale complexion resolved to make herself known to the Sun by sending him a token of her affection.

To this end she asked the man that plays the music to stop playing for a while; then she plucked from the sea of clouds a most brilliant rose-coloured moonstone. Next, with a little gold taken from the dawn sky, she cunningly wrought a splendrous jewel that was the perfect mirror of her love. It had about it a beauty more permanent than the soft lip or flashing eye, a beauty that is for ever and mocks Time.

IF YOU LIKE

AND JOIN US

DANCE IN TIME

IN OUR JIG

When the work was done and the stone was set, the pale and beautiful lady sent for her special messengers, the frog and the hare; the hare because he was as swift as the wind, and the frog for his wisdom, as old as the hills.

"Jack Hare," said she, "listen well. I entrust you with this amulet, and you have but one day to deliver it to my Lord the Sun. Take care, for the way of the little messenger is full of dangers, and yours especially so. Through earth and air and fire and water you must journey, until you reach my Lord the Sun. When you have reached him, show him the jewel and say to him it will be his if he will only give me the answer to this riddle:

"Fifty is my first,
Nothing is my second,
Five just makes my third,
My fourth a vowel is reckoned,

"Now to find my name,
Fit my parts together,
I die if I get cold,
But never fear cold weather.

"Now be off, Jack, and be quick! And you, frog, you must follow Jack's fortune and help him when you can. Although his legs, like yours, are long, his brain is very small and he may falter in this errand."

AND THE SLEEPY

HOURS OF NIGHT

THE DAY BEGINS

ARE OVER

J ack set off with a great bound and a purposeful
expression, pretending he knew exactly where to go
and how to get there. But it wasn't long before he was
most terribly lost and just jogged along muttering to himself,

"Jack, Jack do this, do that, it's always old Jack Hare, on
the go from dusk to dawn, the Hare-bell's always ringing.
Jack be quick and Jack in a box and Jack be in the cellar.
Well ... Jack's as good as his mistress and Ja——— ... "

BUMP!

He was so caught up in his own little troubles that he
hadn't noticed the Penny-Pockets Lady on the road, selling
her fortunes.

"Where's your penny, Long Ears? A penny for your
fortune."

"I've no penny," said Jack.

"No penny? No penny? Then why go bumping into
people? Have you no manners?"

"No—er—yes, I mean—I just want to know which way to
the Sun—er—please."

"If you've no penny then you must answer this riddle:

"I have a little house,
Its windows number plenty,
It's full of flowers that no man picked,
And you may have it when it's empty."

Jack answered directly, as it was so simple, and licked his
lips and whiskers. "Now, which way to the Sun?"

The lady took her hand from her pocket and pointed UP.

AND A COLOUR

FIND THE POCKET

NOW PASS ME BY

CHOOSE A NUMBER

Jack looked up and was astonished to see far above him a tiny figure moving from cloud to cloud. Just then, the being swooped down to hover a few inches above his head.

"Good morning, how did you do?" said Jack, remembering his manners but forgetting his grammar.

"Hello, my name's Tara. Tara Tree-tops. Tara's from the Latin you know, and this is my friend Craw. Isn't he handsome?"

"'Ansome, 'ansome, 'ansome," shrieked Craw, and puffed himself out to show off all his pretty feathers.

Nasty bird, thought Jack, but didn't say so.

"We were looking for lost dreams," said Tara, "they're all there up in the clouds, and when the clouds become too full they fall down again; the nasty ones as hailstorms with thunder, and the nice as gentle rain with rainbows. Most of them are quite boring though, like bishops' dreams of corduroy trousers, and bicycles for prime ministers. But sometimes I'm lucky enough to find the feasts of shipwrecked sailors or the palaces of chambermaids ... What's your dream?"

"I want to find the Sun," said Jack.

"Very well," said Tara, "but first you must hear my riddle:

"I have a little sister
And in the fields she's seen,
Dressed in yellow petticoats,
And a gown of green.
She's not a bird and cannot sing,
But she can fly without a wing.

"Now, jump with me and you may find the Sun behind a cloud."

The little hare jumped for all his worth, and up and up he went, over the tree tops, over the church steeple, and over the clouds — but the higher he got, the smaller the Sun became.

NOT AS HIGH

THE SEA SO DEEP

THE HILLS ARE

AS A DREAM

JACK HARE

IN HASTE TO CHASE

PETALS TUMB

UMPS DOG

ROSE BLUSHING

E UPON AIR

As the hare got close to where the Sun *ought* to be, he heard the most terrible hullabaloo. All the people of earth had taken kettles and pans and sticks and pots, and drums and guns and gongs, and were making a fearful din; and this is the reason why.

The Lady Moon, disregarding all advice given to her by the other celestial bodies, had disobeyed Newton's Universal Law of Gravitation, and instead of continuing her dance in her prescribed orbit, had stayed behind to watch with anticipation the progress of the little hare. It was in thus doing that the unhappy Moon was the instrument of her own undoing. To understand completely, you need to solve this simple riddle:

> I am the beginning of eternity,
> Followed by half a circle, close on by half a square,
> Through my fourth my fifth is seen,
> To be the first in every pair.
> My sixth begins my seventh,
> The end of time and space,
> Now put my parts together to see what's taken place.

When the lady realised what she had done, and saw the hare falling out of the sky and all the other animals running in terror for their lives, she opened her mouth and SCREAMED. A horrible, silent, ghostly scream. The sort of scream that will turn the milk, sour the cream, blight a crop, and lame a horse as it stands in its stall.

All the horrors of the night came forth in this one dreadful scream.

I FOLLOW YOU ROUND AND ROUND AND ROUND AND ROUND

YOU FOLLOW ME

The Sun was gone now and the fingers of shadowy night chilled the air. The shrieking and wailing of the people and the banging of their drums reached a climax. Cold panic gripped the animals, and those that only moments before were the deadliest of enemies ran side by side. The fox and the goose, the owl and the shrew, the cat and the hound ran round and round and round until they turned into one huge zoological pudding!

Even the animals themselves were unable to distinguish one from another … In fact, that's how the animals got their tails, but that's in another story. (See if you can count the animals in the picture opposite and give them all names. The answer is at the bottom of the page.)

Jack's small brain was ill-equipped to deal with such a commotion and it was as much as he could do to remember who he was. To save him from losing his wits entirely, he repeated to himself this, his own little riddle:

"A hopper of ditches,
A cropper of corn,
A little brown deer,
With leathery horn."

This went on until, little by little, the Sun returned and the people, realising that the demon of the night hadn't eaten their Sun after all, stopped the banging and shouting and went back to work.

After carefully disentangling himself from all the other animals, Jack ran off to hide in a tree, just in case it should all happen again.

There are twelve animals:
a cat, a corse, a horse, a dog (saddle-back of course),
a dog, a dow, a cow, a care, a hare, a ham, a ram and a rat

ALL ANIMALS ARE EQUAL IN A TALE FROM TAIL TO TAIL OF TAIL TO TAIL FIND TO END

Now that the eclipse had passed, Jack decided to continue his journey, but just then he heard the strains of a sad and sorrowful tune. Looking out of the tree in which he was hiding, he saw a curious little man sitting upon a hillock, playing a violin. Jack jumped down; the little man was the oldest, most crinkled creature he had ever seen, except for an aged tortoise in Dudley Zoo.

"Good day," said the musician. "I am the man that plays the music that makes the world go round. Can I help you?"

Jack related his story and the man stopped the music. "In my opinion," said he, "you require the assistance of the Practical Man. I am but a poet and a musician. You must go to the town and seek him out. To help you on your way, I shall play the Song of the Sun. The Sun is the eye of day, and as long as I play this tune, the day's eye cannot close again."

The man played the Song of the Sun so sweetly that it made the happy daisies grow, and with the sound of the song in his ears, Jack set off. But when he got to the town, all the shops were closed on account of it being Wednesday and half-day closing. However, there was one dingy little antique shop that stayed open, "so as to catch the passing trade". Jack peered in through the window.

"Step in," said the proprietor through the glass, "I have many treasures of antiquity that will take your fancy, or maybe I can show you an hare-loom or two?"

Oh dear, thought Jack, a humorist.

A ROSE IN MY

FIDDLE DE DE DUM

A DAISY DAY

RIDDLE DE DE

JACK IN

I AM OLD

IC LISTER
MONGER

PUT IN OR

THE GREEN EYE GLASS

ER TO PASS

L.LEVY

Sweet Confectionary

Jack entered the shop.

"Excuse me, sir, are you the Practical Man?"

"Practical! On Wednesday afternoons I could be practically anything. What's up?"

Jack told of his adventures — about the jump, the Sun going out, and the little tortoise-like man. To listen better, the Practical Man took off his glasses and polished them with a red and white spotted handkerchief, but when it came to the bit about GOLD, he popped them on his nose.

"Right!" said he. "I have the solution. Fetch that eye-glass from the window whilst I collect the few other things we'll need."

Moments later, the Practical Man had collected everything in an old cane-back chair. Picking the whole lot up, he waddled out of the shop.

"Come, let us take a little stroll, then some tea, and maybe a little something ... to eat."

Jack followed and they went down the street, along the promenade, and down to the beach. The town was a well-known seaside resort. They walked along the sand until they came to a deserted spot where the man emptied the chair of its contents and flopped himself down in it. "This is just the spot for our experiment. Fetch driftwood and make a pile of it just here." Jack did as he was told.

Taking the magnifying glass, the Practical Man held it over the pile and a tiny sun appeared on one of the sticks, getting hotter and hotter, until, with a PUFF! it burst into flame.

"The Sun's arrived!" cried the Practical Man, pulling a toasting fork from inside his jacket. "Now, my little beauty, jump in." With the sting of the toasting fork in his rump, Jack jumped ...

AT HIGH TEA

WAVE QUENCH FIRE

FIRE BOIL KETTLE

AT HIGH TIDE

At this point, Sir Isaac Newton himself enters the story. By now he is very old and grey, and some of his less good theories have been disproved by the clever men of today, but despite all, his Universal Law of Gravitation still rules everywhere.

Although the Moon had disobeyed his laws, and would therefore have to forfeit the Hare-bell, it seemed unfair that the brave little hare should end up toasted by the Practical Man. Besides, although this may not be the happiest of stories, it is not a tragedy.

When he saw Jack Hare jump towards the fire, and the Practical Man brandishing the toasting fork, Sir Isaac grabbed the strings of gravitational force that bound Jack to his destiny and PULLED ———

Jack was deflected mid-leap, swerved sideways and fell SPLASH into the water. This now completed the Moon's curious instructions. He'd started in the earth, had gone up into the air with Tara Tree-tops, had passed through the fire of the Practical Man, and now here he was in the water.

Down and down he fell into the gloomy depths, until he could hardly see a paw in front of his face.

Then, through the murky waters, he saw a distant yellow light. This must surely be the Sun, thought Jack. To find out what he really saw, answer this slippery riddle:

My first begins first, and I am myself my second. My next is the end of ends, followed by the beginning of hope.
Now put me on one line, and you will find my name,
I live my whole life out of doors, but never feel the rain.

JACK *QUICK*

AND JACK JUMPS

JACK BE NIMBLE

OVER THE FLAME

J ack could see now that it wasn't the Sun after all. "Glood day," said the fish, sounding like someone with a mouthful of cherries.

"Oh," said Jack, "I thought you were my Sun."

"How abslurd."

"No, no," said Jack, "the SUN," and drew a big circle in the water.

"Then why have you come to the blottom of the ocean?"

Dear me, thought Jack, this is going to take all day. I'll flatter him. "Please, oh fish, most worthy, noble and glorious fish, please, fishy most high, can you direct me to the Sun?"

"You've blissed out educated," said the fish conceitedly, "blut I will help you if you can blanswer this riddle:

"What is nothing on its outside,
And nothing on its inside,
Is lighter than a fleather,
But ten men cannot pick it up?"

Jack opened his mouth and out came a bubble! "Correct," said the fish. "Now flollow the frog. He will show you where lives the Spirit of Water. She will tell you how to get to the Sun."

Jack followed the frog and they swam until they came to a sparkling lake, where a charming young lady swam back and forth, measuring its length.

"Next time she passes," said the frog, "ask her."

Jack did, and this was her strange reply:

"Stand at the water's edge a little before the Sun sets in the west, and you will see a yellow carpet. If you can run its length before the Sun has time to set, you will reach your destination. Good luck!"

I HAVE SEEN

IN DEEP WATERS

MY REFLECTION

BLUE AND GREEN

I AM HYDROGEN

CRYSTAL

Already the golden light of late afternoon was colouring the sky, and Jack realised that time was getting short. So, running as fast as his legs would carry him, he set off for the West Country. With not a minute to spare, he reached the shore, and there, spread out over the sea between him and the Sun, was a bright yellow pathway. Without stopping, not even to take breath, the hare LEAPED.

Jack travelled so speedily and reached such a velocity that Sir Isaac Newton and his gravity were forced to let him go. He had now escaped the earth's powerful attraction, and was travelling end over end, through space towards the Sun.

Sir Isaac looked out over the sea and said to himself, "All my life I seem to have been only like a boy playing on the sea-shore and diverting myself in now and then finding a smoother pebble or a prettier shell than ordinary, whilst the great ocean of truth lay all undiscovered before me."

On reaching the Sun, Jack was horrified to find that he no longer had the jewel ... IT WAS GONE!

"Well," said the Sun, with a loud commanding voice, "why have you come here?"

Jack thought quickly, then said, "Great Lord Sun, I bring you a precious gift from a noble and gracious lady, and it would be yours if it were not the answer to this riddle:

"Fifty is my first,
Nothing is my second,
A snake will make my third,
Then three parts a cross is reckoned.
Now to find my name, fit my parts together,
I am all your past, and you fear me in cold weather?"

THE SUN SET AND THE DAY WAS OVER.

A DESTINATION UNDER THE SKY

OVER THE WATER

A CULMINATION

From the start, Mike Barker and John Rousseau saw that they had to find a sentence from the book that *described* the spot as there was no other way of pinpointing it accurately enough. After going up a few blind alleys, they decided that something in the pictures must point to letters in the borders which would spell out the words needed. Here's how they did it.

They began by connecting the *colours* of letters on the paper pinned up above the bell in the Isaac Newton picture to the numbers in the magic square in the Penny-Pockets picture: 1 equals red, 2 yellow, 3 green, 4 blue and so on. The colours on the Penny-Pockets apron confirm this. The Isaac Newton puppets they felt sure were the key. Using their colour sequence, you will see that the string from the red ring of the right hand goes to the longest finger on the left hand of the puppet; the yellow ring connects with the left big toe; the green ring goes to the right longest finger; the blue to the right big toe. Do the same, in the same sequence, with rings on Isaac Newton's left hand and the girl puppet. Behind Isaac Newton all the puppets have rings hanging from feet, fingers or fins. The girl puppet is pointing to her eyes, the other puppets are hanging from their eyes, and it says on the title page, "To solve the hidden riddle, you must use your *eyes*, and find the hare in every picture that may *point* you to the prize." So eyes are the pointers.

Mike and John then drew lines from the left eye through left longest finger, from left eye through left big toe, right eye through right longest finger, right eye through right big toe – to the centre of letters in the border. They applied the method to all creatures (except those shown with *black* rings in the Newton picture) as they appear in all the pictures in turn, where eyes and hands or paws or fins are visible. To get letters in the correct order they used a hierarchy of men, women, children, hares, then other animals, birds, fish or frogs.

By this means they arrived at the sentence: CATHERINES (first picture) /LONG FINGER (second)/OVER (third)/SHADOWS/EARTH/BURIED/YELLOW AMULET/MIDDAY/POINTS/THE/HOUR/IN/LIGHT OF EQUINOX/LOOK YOU. If you arrange these words and phrases one above another, you will see the initials spell CLOSE BY AMPTHILL.

The magic square on the sand in the last picture is the final confirmer. Apply the Penny-Pockets square to it and 1 is 10, 2 is 4/6, 3 is 4, and so on. This refers to the number of letters that make up the word or phrase derived from each picture.

So now you have it all. Well, nearly all. I'll leave you to spot the other confirmers and the lead given by the *Sunday Times* drawing.

K.W.